How to start a new moving company

company

A Step by Step Guide on how to start a new moving company

By Elizabeth King

ISBN-13:978-1534632752

ISBN-10:1534632751

Printed in the United States of America.

Table of Contents

Introduction

First, welcome to your new journey. Not everyone has the ambition to start their own moving company. But you have decided to, so let's get you on the right road.

Most trucking companies fail with in the first 7 months, why? Mostly because they are not prepared for what the road has for them.

It is my intention to pave that road for you.

So, let's get started.

Elizabeth
Previous CEO of Gulf Coast Moving & Storage

Chapter One

Start Up Cost

Alright, so you either currently drive a big truck for a moving company across the country and figure you can do this yourself. Or, you are strong and help friends move, so why not start your own moving company? Whatever the reason is, stay strong in your decision, follow this step by step guide, and you can have a successful company.

Before you get started, you need to ask yourself if you will move locally, across town or will you cross state lines? If you will stay local, you will only need a DOT number but if you cross state lines, you will need to get your motor carrier authority number as well.

We will be covering expenses for local moving companies.

So let's start with making a plan, listing what you will need to have to get started. Some of this will depend on your credit score, unfortunately that is where our world is heading, everything leans on credit score.

1. DOT $300
2. Insurance $4000-6000
3. Company setup $250
4. Fuel - 1 week $500

   Most fuel cards will bill weekly, so you have almost two weeks to start paying.

5. Maintenance-1st mo. $180 – 300

   Oil changes typically cost up to $300, you'll need one about every six weeks

6. Truck letters $90-250
   a. If you are just getting company name, DOT number, VIN number then this will run around $90 but if you wish to have the company name on the box of your truck, it will be several hundred. Remember, name recognition is key when building a company, the more your name is out there, the move calls you will get. I can't tell you how many customers called us because they saw one of our trucks

7. Leadboards $15-60

   I loved working with 123movers.com and received tons of leads

Total amount needed to get started and running:
$ 5000-7500

Business Plan

Putting together a business plan can be simple as a few pages showing what you want to do, how you're going to get started and what your one or three-year plan is for the future of your company.

Most business plans are used to obtain financial backing from banks or even family members. Other business plans can be used to help show the future plan of your company.

Here are some tips in creating a simple business plan:

1. One-line description of your company, service offered
2. Financial model: Start-up cost; expenses, income (potential) *see below for sample*
3. Opportunity: what need will your company provide a solution for? (transportation of household items.)
4. Milestones: Finding/purchasing truck, obtaining authority, ins, etc., opening company date, getting freight
5. Business operation – what tools and resources will you use to run your company? Loadboards to find loads, QuickBooks or something like that for accounting are just a few tools you'll want to look into using.
6. Why are you qualified to succeed – years in industry, this is like your resume
7. Competition – choose 2 of your competitors and list their strengths and weaknesses

Example:

Business Plan

A. Introduction

1. **Name of Company:** _____ **Contact Number:** _____

   Name of Applicant: _____
   (Please provide photo identification with your application)

2. **Is this a new or existing business?**

   ❏ New   ❏ Existing   Date business established: _____

3. **Type of Operation:**

   ❏ Manufacturing   ❏ Wholesale/Retail

   ❏ Agriculture   ❏ Construction

   ❏ Aquaculture / Fishing   ❏ Transportation

   ❏ Forestry   ❏ Mining

   ❏ Tourism   ❏ Other (Specify) _____

4. **Mailing Address:** _____

   Postal Code: _____

5. **Telephone Numbers:**   Residence: _____ Cell: _____

   Fax: _____ E-mail: _____

6. **Proposed location of business:** _____

7. **Legal Form of Business:**

   ❏ Incorporated   ❏ Sole Proprietorship

   ❏ Partnership   ❏ Co-operative

   ❏ To be incorporated

Projected Business Expenses

How much capital are you planning to invest in starting up your trucking company? Also, try to forecast the financial requirements for the first year.

Particulars	Start-up	3 months	6 months	12 months
Authority/DOT				
Insurance				
Legal form of business				
Fuel				
Truck letters				
Load boards				
Accounting/Office Software				

Notes

Chapter Two

What's next? Paperwork

Authority - DOT

Yes, sadly the next step is paperwork, and trust me there is quite a bit of it.

You'll start by going to FMCSA website, click on registration and Getting started:

https://www.fmcsa.dot.gov/registration/getting-started

Here they show you the steps of the registration process.

You can apply for your MC and DOT numbers online.

**Remember to keep your PIN when you first start the application, you'll use this over and over again.

Insurance

Once you've applied for your authority, you have a short period of time to obtain insurance and have the insurance company file the MCS90 form to FMCSA.

When you are first starting out, it's hard to find a good company because most trucking start-ups close their doors with in the first eight months which makes it hard for the one's that will make it.

We used Rig quote, their customer service was excellent and when I told them the budget we had, they found a way to meet it.

Legal Company Setup

This next part is going to be up to you, whether you have no intentions of growing and just want to have your own authority so maybe a DBA (doing business as) works for you. Some may have big dreams about growing and adding trucks and drivers over the next five years to definitely a corporation is the way you should look at going. There's also a LLC which is great for growing companies as well, there are some tax advantages to this form compared to a corporation.

I would suggest discussing with your spouse or accountant to determine what is best for you.

<u>Here are the definitions of each form of legal setup:</u>

Doing Business As: DBAs are also known as Fictitious Names, Fictitious Business Names, Assumed Names, and Trade Names. Essentially, a DBA is the name of a business other than the owner's name or, in the case of a corporation, a name that is different from the legal or true corporate name as on file with the Secretary of State

Corporation: a company or group of people authorized to act as a single entity (legally a person) and recognized as such in law.

LLC: A limited liability company (**LLC**) is the United States-specific form of a private limited company. It is a business structure that combines the pass-through taxation of a partnership or sole proprietorship with the limited liability of a corporation.

Tax ID Number / FEIN

Even if you are a DBA and everything else is under your social security number, you will have to have a tax id number from the IRS. You will use this number for many things, and it will ultimately help your company build credit.

TIN / EIN

You can apply for your tax id or employer identification number online at the IRS website:

https://www.irs.gov/Businesses/Small-Businesses-&-Self-Employed/Apply-for-an-Employer-Identification-Number-(EIN)-Online

Notes

_____

_____

_____

_____

_____

_____

_____

_____

_____

_____

_____

_____

Chapter Three

Fuel Cards

There are many options of which fuel card to apply for. Depending on what part of the country you will spend most of your time, could determine whether you go with Wright Express, Fuelman, FleetOne or go directly to the fuel station like with Kangaroo or Pilot.

Each company offers a discount, whether at the pump, when you are billed or quarterly.

There are a variety of ways of being billed and paying. Most companies will set you up on auto draft, or give you a login to their website and you control when you pay them.

*Warning, if you don't pay the bill they will freeze your account and turn off your card until paid.

Software Needs

If you want to run your business correctly, I would suggest getting a QuickBooks, Quicken, or Money program to keep track of where your money is going. This will be helpful when you file taxes. You can get an old fashion disk or some offer online programs.

There are many load boards to choose from. My favorite and easiest to work with was 123movers.com.

Notes

_____

_____

_____

_____

_____

_____

_____

_____

_____

_____

_____

_____

_____

_____

Chapter Four

Necessary Marketing Tools

Word of mouth is the best marketing tool.

Start a facebook page – you can share with your friends who will share with their friends and get your name out.

Your company name on your truck is also a great marketing tool.

Having a website is fairly inexpensive and can be easy to do. Check out vistaprint.com and godaddy.com for reasonable prices and easy to setup websites.

Don't grow too fast

Speaking from experience, the more trucks you buy, the more labor cost you have and fuel cost. Make sure you are running smoothly before buying a second truck. Also, there are great rental companies out there if you need a second truck in a pinch, we used Penske and you can get a magnet for the truck door with your company name and DOT number, you can get that from vistaprint.com also.

Notes

_____

_____

_____

_____

_____

_____

_____

_____

_____

_____

_____

_____

_____

_____

Chapter Five

Equipment

A 26' box truck will handle all your large three to four bedroom moves. However, a smaller 14' box truck is also great for small moves and quick money.

We purchased used equipment to get started, reasonably priced and if you are mechanically inclined then it's a no brainer to buy used at first.

Bidding Jobs

If you have been in the business for many years and you are good at your job, then bidding jobs and making money will be easy for you. But if you are new here are some tips:

1) Check out your competition, how are they quoting? Are they hourly only? Do they have packages based on the size of the home (i.e. number of bedrooms).? Do they have a minimum? Are they charging for fuel?
2) Either make an appointment to visit your potential client and walk through the house or office that is being move.
3) Make an inventory of all that will be moved.
4) You'll want to have an idea of the hourly rate you want to charge whether per hour or in a package. A rate that will cover all your overhead and in the future give you a profit.

Notes

Chapter Six

Drivers, DOT Regulation, Vehicle maintenance

As a wife of a truck driver with over twenty years' experience on the road, I didn't know what I was getting into when we started our own moving company in 2007. One thing I was unclear of was all that was needed to have on file for the driver, or drivers and what the DOT regulation says.

You'll need a file for each driver that includes the following DRIVER QUALIFICATION FILE

1. Employment application
2. Safety performance history record request (below)
3. Motor Vehicle report – MVR (last 3 years)
4. Annual review of MVR/driving record (below)
5. Driver certification of violations (below)
6. Road test (below)
7. Medical certificate
8. Driver daily logs (these can be purchased at truck stops)
9. Vehicle maintenance records (below); NOTE it is not enough just to keep receipts, the FMCSA requires you to record when parts are installed. You can use a simple notebook or I've attached a sample form
10. Pre-employment and random drug test participation and results.

You will need to have a drug/alcohol policy in force as well. I've attached a sample copy of such policy.

SAFETY PERFORMANCE HISTORY RECORDS REQUEST

SECTION 1 — AUTHORIZATION

I, (Print Name) _____, hereby authorize:

(First, M.I., Last)

Previous Employer: _____   Email: _____

Street Address: _____   Phone: _____

City, State, Zip: _____   Fax: _____

to release and forward the information requested by section 3 of this document concerning my Alcohol and Controlled Substance Testing records within the previous 3 years from_____

to: _____   (Date of Employment Application)

Prospective Employer: _____   Attn.: _____

Street Address: _____   Phone: _____

City, State, Zip: _____

In compliance with 49 CFR §§40.25(g) and 391.23(h), release of this information must be made in a written form that ensures confidentiality, such as fax, email, or letter.

Prospective employer's confidential fax number:_____

Prospective employer's confidential email:_____

_____   _____
Applicant's Signature   Date

This information is being requested in compliance with 49 CFR §§ 40.25 and 391.23.

SECTION 2 — ACCIDENT HISTORY

The applicant named above was employed by us.   ☐ Yes   ☐ No

Employed as _____ from (mm/yy) _____ to (mm/yy) _____.

Did he/she drive motor vehicle for you? ☐ Yes ☐ No If yes, what type? ☐ Straight Truck   ☐ Tractor/Semitrailer

☐ Bus   ☐ Cargo Tank   ☐ Doubles/Triples   ☐ Other (Specify) _____

ACCIDENTS: Complete the following for any accidents included on your accident registrar (§390.15(b)) that involved the applicant in the 3 years prior to the application date shown above, or check here ☐ if there is no accident register data for this driver.

Date	Location	No. of Injuries	No. of Fatalities	Hazmat Spill
1._____	_____	_____	_____	_____
2._____	_____	_____	_____	_____
3._____	_____	_____	_____	_____

Please provide information concerning any other accidents involving the applicant that were reported to government agencies or insurers or retained under internal company policies: _____

_____

_____

Signature:_____

Title: _____   Date:_____

PREVIOUS EMPLOYER – COMPLETE SIDE 2, SECTION 3

SECTION 3	**DRUG AND ALCOHOL HISTORY**

If driver was not subject to Department of Transportation testing requirements while employed by this employer, please check here ☐.

	YES	NO
1. Has this person had an alcohol test with a result of 0.04 or higher alcohol concentration?	☐	☐
2. Has this person tested positive or adulterated or substituted a test specimen for controlled substances?	☐	☐
3. Has this person refused to submit to post-accident, random, reasonable suspicion, or follow-up alcohol or controlled substance test?	☐	☐
4. Has this person committed other violations of Subpart B or Part 382 or Part 40?	☐	☐
5. If this person has violated a DOT drug and alcohol regulation, did this person fail to undertake or or complete a program prescribed by a Substance Abuse Professional (SAP) in your employ If yes, please end documentation back with this form.	☐	☐
6. For a driver who successfully completed a SAP's rehabilitation referral and remained in your employ, did this driver subsequently have an alcohol test result of 0.04 or greater, a verified positive drug test, or refuse to be tested?	☐	☐

In answering these questions, include any required DOT drug or alcohol testing information obtained from prior previous employers in the previous 3 years prior to the application date shown on side 1.

Name: _____

Company: _____

Street: _____

City, State, Zip: _____ Phone:_____

Section 3 completed by (Signature)_____ Date:_____

SECTION 4	**MODE OF COMMUNICATION**

This form was sent to previous employer via (check one) ☐ Fax ☐ Mail ☐ Email ☐ Other _____

By _____ Date:_____

SECTION 5	**RECEIPT INFORMATION**

Complete the following when the requested information is obtained.

Information received from_____

Recorded by:_____ Method: ☐ Fax ☐ Mail ☐ Email ☐ Phone

Date:_____ ☐ Other _____

INSTRUCTIONS FOR COMPLETING THE SAFETY PERFORMANCE HISTORY RECORDS REQUEST

SIDE 1 SECTION 1: *Prospective Employee*

- Complete the information required in this section
- Sign and date
- Submit to the prospective employer

SIDE 1 SECTION 2: *Previous Employer*

- Complete the information required in this section
- Sign and date
- Turn form over to complete SIDE 2 SECTION 3

SIDE 2 SECTION 3: *Previous Employer*

- Complete the information required in this section
- Sign and date
- Return to prospective employer

SIDE 2 SECTION 4: *Prospective Employer*

- Verify that prospective employee has correctly completed SIDE 1 SECTION 1

- Complete the information required in this section
- Make a copy of this form and keep it on file
- Send to previous employer

SIDE 2 SECTION 5: *Prospective Employer*

- Record receipt of the information in SECTION 5
- Keep form on file for duration of the driver's employment and for three years thereafter

U. S. DEPARTMENT OF TRANSPORTATION
MOTOR CARRIER SAFETY PROGRAM
ANNUAL REVIEW OF DRIVING RECORD
(49 CFR 391.25)

Name of Motor Carrier: _____

_____   _____
(Name of driver)   (Social Security Number)

    This day I reviewed the driving record of the above named driver in accordance with
CFR 391.25 of the Motor Carrier Safety Regulations. I considered any evidence that the
driver has violated applicable provisions of the MCS Regulations and the Hazardous
Materials Regulations. I considered the driver's accident record and any evidence that
he/she has violated laws governing the operation of motor vehicles, and gave great
weight to violations, such as speeding, reckless driving and operation while under the
influence of alcohol or drugs, that indicate that the driver has exhibited a disregard for the
safety of the public. Having done the above, I find that

[ ] The driver meets the minimum requirements for safe driving, or

[ ] The driver is disqualified to drive a motor vehicle pursuant to CFR 391.15

_____   _____
Date of review   Reviewed by: Signature and Title

MOTOR VEHICLE DRIVER
CERTIFICATION OF VIOLATIONS 391.27

I CERTIFY THAT THE FOLLOWING IS A TRUE AND COMPLETE LIST OF TRAFFIC VIOLATIONS (other than parking violations) FOR WHICH I HAVE BEEN CONVICTED OF OR FORFEITED BOND OR COLLATERAL DURING THE PAST 12 MONTHS.

DATE	OFFENSE	LOCATION	TYPE VEHICLE OPERATED

If no violations are listed above, I certify that I have not been convicted or forfeited bond or collateral on account of any violation required to be listed during the past 12 months.

_____
(Date of Certification)

_____
(Driver's Signature)

_____
(Carrier's Name)

_____
(Motor Carrier's Address)

_____
(Reviewed by: Signature)

_____
(Title)

CERTIFICATE OF DRIVER'S ROAD TEST

Instructions: If the road test is successfully completed, the person who gave it shall complete a certificate of the driver's road test. The original or a copy of the certificate shall be retained in the employing motor carrier's driver qualification file of the person examined and a copy given to the person who was examined. (49CFR 391.31 (e) (f) (g).

CERTIFICATION OF DRIVER ROAD TEST

Driver Name _____

Social Security Number _____

Operator or Chauffeur's License Number _____

State _____

Type of Power Unit _____

Type of Trailer _____

If passenger Carrier, Type of Bus _____

THIS IS TO CERTIFY THAT THE ABOVE NAMED DRIVER WAS GIVEN A ROAD TEST UNDER MY SUPERVISION ON _____, 20_____, CONSISTING OF APPROXIMATELY _____

MILES OF DRIVING. IT IS MY CONSIDERED OPINION THAT THIS DRIVER POSSESSES SUFFICIENT DRIVING SKILL TO OPERATE SAFELY THE TYPE OF COMMERCIAL VEHICLE LISTED ABOVE.

_____   _____
(SIGNATURE OF EXAMINER)   (TITLE)

_____
(ORGANIZATION AND ADDRESS OF EXAMINER)

Inspection, Repair & Maintenance Record

VEHICLE IDENTIFICATION

MAKE	SERIAL NUMBER
YEAR	TIRE SIZE
COMPANY NUMBER/OTHER I.D.	OWNER, IF LEASED

DATE: . MILEAGE   OPERATION PERFORMED, INSPECTION OR REPAIRS

Model Substance Abuse Policy

I pledge that my company will take reasonable action to create and maintain a workplace free from substance abuse. My company will work to increase awareness of the dangers of substance abuse within our workplace and throughout the construction industry.

TABLE OF CONTENTS

SCOPE OF POLICY

This document contains procedures for implementing a drug and alcohol testing program at the *Company*. The company prohibits the use, possession, sale, purchase, manufacture, distribution, transfer or consumption of alcohol and all illegal drugs, including legally regulated drugs.

This program applies to all employees and potential employees of the company, as well as subcontractors at all tiers, including non-bargaining and bargaining unit employees.

DEFINITIONS

Banned Substances: Illegal substances, as defined by federal/state laws, including:

    a. Amphetamines
    b. Opiates
    c. Phencyclidine (PCP)
    d. Cocaine
    e. THC (Marijuana/Cannabinoids)
    f. Intoxicants (drug and alcohol)
    g. Synthetic drugs

Third-Party Administrator: The company may retain a third-party administrator to perform testing and reporting procedures. See Appendix A: Additional Definitions.

POLICIES AND PROCEDURES

A urine drug screen shall be administered under the following circumstances.

1. **Pre-Hire Drug Screening**. All potential employees must submit to a urine drug screen no later than the commencement of employment. Pre-hire drug screening will test for the presence of illegal drugs and substances and the illegal use of prescription drugs. This screen does not include an alcohol test. Potential employees who refuse to submit to this test will not be permitted to work for the company.

If the employer participates in a pre-screen/certification program through a collective bargaining agreement (CBA) or other arrangement, and the potential employee has undergone a prior screening to which, through the CBA or other arrangement, the company is provided access to the results/certification, then the potential employee shall be deemed to have complied with the company's pre-hire drug screening requirements.

2. **Existing Employees**. Existing employees who are transferred from another location must submit to a urine drug screen prior to entering the jobsite. This screen tests for the presence of illegal drugs and substances and the illegal use of prescription drugs. This screen does not include an alcohol test. Employees who refuse to submit to this test will not be permitted to work for the company.

If the employer participates in a pre-screen/certification program through a CBA or other arrangement, and the employee has undergone a prior screening to which the company has access to the results/certification, then the employee shall be deemed to have complied with the company's pre-hire drug screening requirements. Likewise, if an employee has undergone a urine drug screen with the company within the previous three (3) months, and the company deems this test sufficient, then the employee shall be deemed to have complied with the company's pre-hire drug screening requirements.

3. **Testing for Cause**. All employees may be tested for cause when a reasonable suspicion exists that the employee appears to be under the influence of illegal drugs or illegally using prescription drugs, synthetic drugs and/or alcohol.

4. **Causal/Incident-Related.** All employees who are involved with, or may have contributed to, an incident that results in property damage or requires treatment beyond onsite first aid are required to submit to a drug screen and alcohol test. (Note: a company may also require a drug screen and/or alcohol test for incidents resulting in first aid treatment. Please consult your state/local laws pertaining to testing procedures to verify if such a practice is permissible).

5. **Random.** When permitted by law, employees may be randomly selected for unannounced drug and alcohol screening using a scientifically/statistically valid computerized number generation process. Employees are notified of selection no more than 48 hours prior to testing.

6. **Reinstatement, Return-to-Duty and Follow-Up Testing.** After signing an agreement or participating in substance abuse counseling established by the company, the employee must complete a drug screen before returning to active employment.

TESTING PROCEDURES

I. Drug Screening of Applicants for Employment

1. Upon entering the jobsite or workplace, all applicants will proceed to the project office or trailer. They will be advised whether specimen collection will occur onsite in an approved facility or at an approved clinic offsite.

2. Each applicant will read and sign a Drug Screen Consent Form prior to any test being administered.

3. On a pre-printed, itemized form furnished by the employer, each applicant will be asked to identify any medication he/she is taking or has taken during the 30 days preceding the test.

4. A formal chain of custody will be established for every drug screen.

5. A split sample consisting of two urine collection containers sealed in a plastic container will be furnished to the applicant. (Note: Testing may be performed by a third-party administrator.) The containers must contain an amount of urine sufficient for one

Enzyme Medical Immunoassay Test (EMIT) and two Gas Chromatography/Mass Spectrometry (GC/MS) tests (no less than 2 ounces of urine per container). Each applicant's urine specimen will be collected and temperature tested for verification. The second container will be used in the event the first container becomes contaminated.

6. Before the specimen leaves the applicant's sight, the urine containers will be sealed with security tape that has been initialed by applicant.

7. Specimens collected onsite will be transported to a laboratory in accordance with the chain of custody procedures. A portion of the sample will be tested using the EMIT; if positive, another portion and/or the split sample will be tested for verification using the GC/MS test.

8. The remainder of the urine specimen and split sample will remain at the laboratory for 30 days following the test.

9. Upon signing a form giving consent to use the urine sample for drug screening, the applicant is eligible for employment on a 72-hour probationary basis. This consent form is co-signed by the collection specialist.

10. Any applicant who refuses to submit to a drug screening will not be eligible for employment.

11. The employer receives the drug test results within 72 hours. If the applicant's test results in a confirmed positive, as confirmed by a medical review officer (MRO), he/she will be terminated immediately and paid for all hours worked, if permissible by state/local law. The individual will not be eligible for employment with the employer for a period to be determined by the employer, not exceeding one year. If hired later by the employer, and contingent on a negative drug screen, the employee may be tested periodically without notice for a period of up to one year from the date of hire.

12. If any individual who has tested positive by the MRO wants to confirm the results of the GC/MS test, he/she may do so by having a GC/MS test performed on the previously collected split urine specimen at a certified National Institute on Drug Abuse (NIDA) or Substance Abuse and Mental Health Services Administration (SAMHSA) laboratory of his/her choice. The specimen will be shipped directly from the employer's lab to the lab of the employee's choice. The costs of this test will be borne by the employee. If the results of this test are negative, the individual will be reinstated with full back pay and benefits, and will be reimbursed for the cost of the test. The individual must exercise the option of a second GC/MS test within 24 hours of being notified of the positive results.

13. Pre hire drug screens include tests for at least the following (a five-panel drug screen):

   a) Amphetamines
   b) Opiates
   c) Phencyclidine (PCP)
   d) Cocaine
   e) THC (Marijuana/Cannabinoids)

The company reserves the right to administer testing for additional substances (For more information on seven-panel, 10-panel, 12-panel and hair follicle tests, refer to the "Best

Practices" section of the Construction Coalition for a Drug- and Alcohol-Free Workplace website at www.drugfreeconstruction.org).

II. Drug Screening of Transferred Employees

The procedure for testing employees transferred from another jobsite is the same as the pre-hire procedure.

III. "For Cause" Testing Procedures

1. All employees working for the company may be tested for illegal drugs, substances, synthetic drugs and alcohol if there is reasonable suspicion that the employee is under the influence of alcohol, any of the substances identified in paragraph 13 or abuse of prescription medication. For the purpose of this program, the term "reasonable suspicion" shall be defined as "aberrant behavior or unusual on-duty behavior of an individual employee who:

    (a) is observed on duty by either the employee's immediate supervisor, higher ranking employee, or other managerial personnel who have been trained to recognize the symptoms of drug abuse, impairment or intoxication (observations shall be documented by the observers);

    (b) exhibits the type of behavior that shows accepted symptoms of intoxication or impairment caused by controlled substances or alcohol or addiction to or dependence upon said controlled substances; and

    (c) such conduct cannot reasonably be explained by other causes such as fatigue, lack of sleep, side effect of prescription or over-the-counter medications, illness, reaction to noxious fumes or smoke.

2. Testing of this type will not be conducted without the written approval of the company's superintendent or designated manager. The jobsite superintendent or designated manager must document in writing who is to be tested and why the test was ordered, including the specific objective facts constituting reasonable suspicion leading to the test being ordered, and the name of any source(s) of this information. One copy of this document shall be given to the employee before he/she is required to be tested. After receiving a copy of the document, the affected employee shall be given enough time to read the document.

3. When a supervisor, higher ranking employee or other managerial personnel has reasonable suspicion to believe an employee is using, consuming or under the influence of an alcoholic beverage, non-prescription controlled substance (other than over-the-counter medication), and/or non-prescribed narcotic drug while on duty, that person will notify the jobsite superintendent or designated manager for the purpose of observation and confirmation of the employee's condition. The employee will be given an opportunity to explain his/her condition, such as reaction to a prescribed drug, fatigue, lack of sleep, exposure to noxious fumes, reaction to over-the-counter medication or illness. If, after this explanation, the jobsite superintendent or designated manager continues to have

reasonable suspicion that the employee is using, consuming and/or under the influence of an alcoholic beverage, non-prescribed controlled substance or non-prescribed narcotic while on duty, then, by a written order signed by the superintendent or designated manager, the employee may be ordered to immediately submit to a drug and alcohol screen. Refusal to submit to testing after being ordered to do so may result in disciplinary action up to and including discharge.

4. Employee drug screens for cause will include testing for alcohol, as well as the same drugs as the pre-hire screening test. Each employee will read and execute a consent form prior to any test being administered. Failure to execute the consent form will result in termination.

5. Reasonable suspicion testing shall be performed at a NIDA/SAMHSA-approved clinic. The individual will be immediately accompanied to the clinic by a company representative. Samples will be taken as per the pre-hire procedure.

6. An EMIT test and, if positive, a confirming GC/MS test, will be performed on the urine sample. The remainder of the sample and the split sample will be stored at the laboratory for 30 days.

7. If an employee's test is positive, his/her employment will be terminated immediately. The employee will be given a copy of the results of the drug screen. He/she may have the second container tested at his/her own expense as per the pre-hire procedure.

8. Alcohol detection will be based on an evidential breath alcohol device approved by the National Highway Traffic Safety Act. If an employee's test results indicate he/she is legally intoxicated at or above the state of jurisdiction's legal limit, he/she may be subject to discipline up to and including discharge.

IV. Causal/Incident-Related Testing

Subject to applicable law and consistent with reasonable suspicion, the company reserves the right to require its employees to present themselves for testing within 24 hours following an employee's involvement in an accident, near accident or an incident resulting in lost work time, property damage, and/or injury to any employee or other person while on the company's premises, on the job or otherwise working for the company.

V. Random Testing

Subject to applicable law, the company reserves the right to require its employees to present themselves for random, unannounced testing. The company will adopt an objective procedure, using a statistically valid number generation process, to randomly select employees to be tested. Upon anonymous selection, the company will notify the employee(s) to report immediately for drug testing. The company solely determines the time and frequency of random drug tests. Any employee may be selected for random testing in accordance with state/local laws. An employee could be randomly selected for testing more than once a year.

VI. Reinstatement, Return-to-Duty and Follow-Up Testing/Rehabilitation Programs

The company maintains a referral relationship with drug and alcohol abuse services. Additionally, certain health insurance benefits may provide help to employees who suffer from substance abuse and/or other personal or emotional problems; however, it is the responsibility of each employee to seek necessary professional assistance before alcohol and drug problems lead to disciplinary action.

If the company mandates a sponsored rehabilitation program, the employee will be subjected to a drug screen following the procedures outlined in Section I (Drug Screening of Applicants for Employment) prior to reinstatement. In addition, per post-rehabilitation program monitoring guidelines, the company may subject the employee to follow-up testing for a period to be determined in cooperation with the rehabilitation program and employer. Testing will follow the procedures outlined in Section V (Random Testing).

VII. Drug and Alcohol Testing Requirements for Employees with a Commercial Driver's License (CDL)

The United States Department of Transportation (DOT) requires that all employees maintaining a CDL and operating commercial motor vehicles be subjected to the drug screen policies outlined in the "Testing Procedures" section of this document. CDL employees, per the DOT, are required to submit to a minimum five-panel drug screen for the presence of:

1. Amphetamines
2. Opiates
3. Phencyclidine (PCP)
4. Cocaine
5. THC (Marijuana/Cannabinoids)

A positive test result requires the employee to be immediately removed from operating any commercial motor vehicles on public roadways. In addition, employees whose test produces a positive result must complete return-to-duty and follow-up testing after completion of an approved rehabilitation program as prescribed by a substance abuse professional. Follow-up testing must include a minimum of six unannounced, directly observed drug screens within 12 months of the initial return-to-duty screen following the procedures outlined in Section V (Random Testing).

For more information on the DOT's CDL drug screening requirements, visit:
http://www.fmcsa.dot.gov/documents/Drug_Alcohol_Test_Brochure2009_508compliant_rev2.pdf

VIII. Disciplinary Policies and Procedures

For examples of disciplinary procedures and appeals processes, visit the "Best Practices" section of the Construction Coalition for a Drug- and Alcohol-Free Workplace website at www.drugfreeconstruction.com.

First Offense

Disciplinary actions defined by the company.

Second Offense

Disciplinary actions defined by the company.

Appealing Disciplinary Action

Appeals process defined by the company.

Substance Abuse Rehabilitation

Following a positive result, the company retains the right to enter the employee into an approved substance abuse rehabilitation program. Upon completion of the program, the employee will be subjected to drug screening procedures outlined in Section VI (Reinstatement, Return-to-Duty and Follow-Up Testing/Rehabilitation Programs).

IX. Policy Amendments

Review Procedures

The company will undertake a comprehensive review of the policy biennially. A review panel consisting of senior management, safety professionals and site employees will assess the relevance and current status of the policy's components, as well as incorporate updated procedures and requirements that will ensure the policy meets or exceeds industry requirements. Any policy changes made as a result of the review will be made available and provided to every employee as an addendum to the company's Employment Policies and Procedures Handbook.

In addition to the biennial policy update, the company may undertake revisions due to new regulatory requirements. Any revisions made outside the biennial review will be provided as a separate addendum to all employees.

X. Confidentiality Statement

Employee information, including drug screen results and rehabilitative programs, will be treated as medical records and will remain strictly confidential following HIPAA guidelines for patient confidentiality. Employee requests to release the results of drug screens to any party outside the company must be made in writing and given to the employee's immediate supervisor and designated safety and health officer.

SAMPLE CONSENT FORM

Pre Hire

_____ Release form for obtaining urine samples for drug screening and permission to furnish the results to the company.

For Cause

_____ Release form for obtaining urine samples for drug screening and permission to furnish the results to the company.

_____ Release form for obtaining NHTSA-approved evidential breath alcohol test and permission to furnish the results to the company.

Post Incident

_____ Release form for obtaining test samples for drug and alcohol screening following any incident requiring medical care.

I hereby authorize the *Company*, its physicians or agents, to take the indicated sample from me to use for the purposes indicated above. I understand why these samples are being requested and I give permission for the results to be released to the company and to my employer (if different).

I further release and hold harmless the owner, the company and its subcontractors from any consequences arising out of the drug and/or alcohol test or results therefrom.

_____

Name   (please print)   Social Security Number

_____

Signature (required)   Date

_____

Street   City   State   Zip

_____

Phone Number (with area code)

_____

Witness   Date

_____

Employer   Occupation

Pre-employment and Random Drug Program

Every driver will need to take a pre-employment drug test and random drug/alcohol test.

There are many, many options of what company to go through to setup your drug program needed by DOT regulations. Most will also provide the necessary supervisory training you will need to complete as well if your spouse or someone else is helping you run the company or you have more than one driver.

Just do a google search and many companies come up. We used our local Workforce Essentials program through our community workforce office. I prefer to support our local companies versus a big company that is based in another state. But that's just me and you have a choice of what you want to do.

Notes

_____

_____

_____

_____

_____

_____

_____

_____

_____

_____

_____

_____

_____

Chapter Seven

What to expect the first year

Your first year will be filled with ups and downs.

What you deal with will depend on what part of the country you are hauling for, what time of the year you start your company and what you are hauling.

Overall, the peak season for this industry starts in March and goes until about the end of October, that is when you will find the best rates for moving freight. During the off peak months, November to February, you will find cheap freight all over the country and no matter what type of equipment you are using.

We typically shut down, or run part time during the off peak season. In the future, we will be closed two weeks around Christmas and the entire week of Thanksgiving. Shippers typically are not hauling during this time and freight is hard to find.

Safety Audit

Within your first year of business, you will have to complete a safety audit. This will vary state to state as how they perform the audit. You may receive an email to go online, like South Carolina does, and submit all your paperwork via an online portal, then DOT will contact you as soon as it is complete to advise if you passed or failed. Or, like Tennessee, you may get a phone call to go to the closest highway patrol office to perform the audit. Currently in TN, there are three locations due to several officers retiring recently, I had to drive two hours for our audit.

The safety audit is to make sure you are running your company like FMCSA and DOT regulate. You'll need to provide the following to them:

1. Company information (what you completed on the FMCSA application)
2. Driver list (see below)
   a. Current and terminated
3. Driver qualification files (list above in chapter six)
4. Alcohol/drug company policy (sample above)
5. Pre-employment and random drug test results and drug program contract
6. Daily log books – they will pull at random one month to review
7. Driver payroll records
8. Driver supporting documents (trip reports, expense records, fuel, toll, scales)
9. Vehicle accident files
10. Vehicle list (make, model, year, VIN) (see below)
11. Vehicle maintenance records
12. Driver vehicle inspection reports (does not apply to one truck operation)
13. Company gross revenue for last full year

14. Total fleet mileage for last full four quarters
15. Form MCS-90 from your insurance company on the current policy

When you get the call or email about the safety audit, they will send you a list of what they need.

The following will help make sure you are prepared when the call comes.

The safety audit is pass or fail, they are looking to make sure you are running the company as you should. If you fail, they will keep a sharp eye on you moving forward and you will have to rectify whatever you failed.

They have several criteria that sends up red flags. They watch the DOT inspections and companies that are shut down. If you do anything out of line, let's say your driver gets shut down over and over for log book entry, that will give them a red flag. Or if you have a driver that has several accidents in a year, that will give them a red flag and the next step would be for them to knock on your door and dig even deeper into your files.

So, keep your nose clean, and you should only hear from them once to perform the safety audit.

Company Data:

USDOT Number: _____

Company name: _____

List all drivers in past 365 days, include company/leased/owner operators:

Driver list for _____ **(carrier)**

Driver Name, Driver's license number, Date of hire, Full/Part time, Termination date

    1. _____

       _____

    2. _____

       _____

Vehicle list for _____ **(carrier)**

Vehicle year, Make, Company unit#, VIN, GVWR

    1. _____

       _____

    2. _____

       _____

List of corporate offices and date of incorporation:

_____

List of all cargo hauled, include hazardous materials:

_____

List number of accidents in past year: _____

List the total fleet mileage for past four quarters: _____

List Gross Revenue for last full fiscal year: _____ for fiscal year ending _____

Company email: _____

Federal Tax ID Number: _____

Above reported by: _____ _____ _____

                (Name)   (Title)   (Date)

Conclusion

Well, that's all I've got to share with you. I hope you found this book useful and easy to help you with starting up and running your new trucking company.

I welcome you to the industry and wish you much success in this new adventure for you.

I'd love to hear from you, how helpful this book was, how easy it was to use to get you started and your story.

Feel free to share by sending me an email at:

liz@evadesante.com

Thanks and God Bless!

19572395R00026